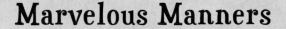

Marvelous Manners

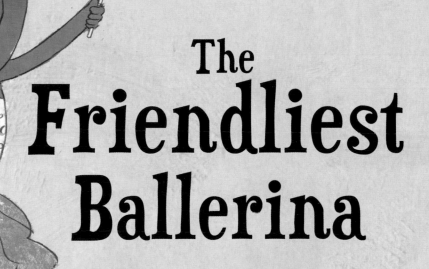

The Friendliest Ballerina

Timothy Knapman

Illustrated by **Jimothy Oliver**

QEB Publishing

Bella **loves** her ballet class—
she's the **best** dancer by far.

Today they have got a show to prepare,
and **Bella** will be the star.

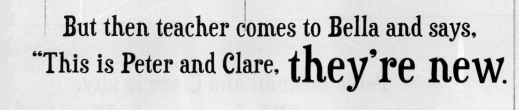

But then teacher comes to Bella and says,
"This is Peter and Clare, **they're new**.

Bella, would you **take care** of them
and show them what they should do?"

Peter is small and Clare is shy,
so Bella says, "Welcome! Hello!

"I'm **so glad** you've joined us—it's just the right time.
You'll both get to be in **our show!**"

Bella **shows** them where to hang up their coats,
she **tells** them what everything's for.

She **helps** them **make friends** with everyone else;
she couldn't do anything more!

But **not long ago**, if you'd asked for her **help**,
Bella would have said, "Sorry, **but no!**"

"I'm **far too busy** to **help** anyone— you see, I am the **star** of the **show!**"

Back then she danced in the **spotlight**,
where she shone like a star—**on her own**.

But **after** the show, when the lights had gone out,
Bella felt **sad** and **alone**.

"Of course!" Bella thought. "How silly I've been!
Being happy or sad all depends,
not on being the star of the show,
but on whether you have any friends!"

So **NOW** look at Bella—how **happy** she is,
as she dances with Peter and Clare!

Peter is small, but he jumps very **high**,
while Clare **spins** and **twirls** everywhere.

Then in no time, it seems, it's the **night** of the show—
Bella's **nervously** waiting to start.

Then Clare comes along and gives Bella a **hug** and a **"thank you"** that warms Bella's heart.

Bella **springs** out on stage, and she dances so well
that the mommies and daddies all **cheer**.

Bella's never been better, and we know why—
it's because her **two friends are near**.

It's good to be the star of the show,
but **remember** how our story ends.

Next Steps

★ After reading the story, have another look at the front cover of the book together. Ask your child to describe the picture of the girl. Discuss what she is doing and what she is wearing.

★ Ask your child whether they like to dance. At this point, it would be good to talk about ballet and describe the picture on the first page.

★ Talk about why Bella enjoyed her dance class.

★ Bella used to feel sad and lonely. Ask your child what made her feel that way. Then discuss why Bella changed the way she treated others. Explain that to be happy, Bella needed to make friends—and not just be a good dancer.

★ Ask your child what Clare did to warm Bella's heart. How does your child feel when they get a hug from a friend?

★ Emphasize that to have fun and to avoid feeling sad and lonely, your child should be friendly and helpful toward other children. Tell them that it's fun and exciting to meet new people and make new friends and that they could even try fun activities with their friends, such as dancing.

★ Ask your child to draw a picture of them dancing alone and another picture of them dancing with their friends. Discuss the different feelings that they may have when they dance alone and when they dance with friends.

Consultant: Cecilia A. Essau
Editor: Alexandra Koken
Designer: Andrew Crowson

Copyright © QEB Publishing 2012

First published in the United States by
QEB Publishing, Inc.
3 Wrigley, Suite A
Irvine, CA 92618

www.qed-publishing.co.uk

ISBN 978 1 60992 344 0

Printed in China

Library of Congress Cataloging-in-Publication Data

Knapman, Timothy.
The friendliest ballerina / by Timothy Knapman ; illustrated by Jimothy Rovolio.
   p. cm. -- (Marvelous manners)
 Summary: Bella, the star of her ballet class, has learned the hard way the importance of being helpful and friendly.
 ISBN 978-1-60992-268-9 (hardcover, library bound)
 [1. Stories in rhyme. 2. Helpfulness--Fiction. 3. Friendship--Fiction. 4. Ballet dancing--Fiction.] I. Rovolio, Jimothy, ill. II. Title.
 PZ8.3.K73Fri 2013
 [E]--dc23
                                        2011051880

McGRAW-HILL READING

Macmillan/McGraw-Hill

A Division of The McGraw·Hill Companies

ISBN 0-02-185281-2

99701

9 780021 852819

5.U.6

P7-EFP-351

Story Questions and Activity

1. How did trumpeter swans almost become extinct?
2. Why did Isabelle, Sidney, and Yo-Yo follow the ultralight plane?
3. Why do you think scientists and bird lovers are working so hard to bring back trumpeter swans?
4. What is the main idea of the book?
5. What about this story relates to *Amistad Rising*? Explain your answer.

More Research

At your school or local library, find the book *The Trumpet of the Swan* by E.B. White. Read it and write a one-page book report about it.

Day after day he pored over his pictures, searching for Planet X. Five years went by and still Clyde could not find it.

Then one day Clyde noticed in his pictures one very faint star with other stars all around it. In one picture it was in one place, and in another picture it was somewhere else.

Lowell Observatory

Observation Circular

THE DISCOVERY OF A SOLAR SYSTEM BODY APPARENTLY TRANS-NEPTUNIAN

Flagstaff, Arizona
March 13, 1930

Systematic search begun years ago supplementing Lowell's investigations for TransNeptunian planet has revealed object which since seven weeks has in rate of motion and path consistently conformed to TransNeptunian body at approximate distance be assigned. Fifteenth magnitude, Position March twelve days three hours GMT was seven seconds of time West from Delta Geminorum, agreeing with Lowell's predicted longitude.

The finding of this object was a direct result of the search program set going in 1905 by Dr. Lowell in connection with his theoretical work on the dynamical evidence of a planet beyond Neptune. The earlier searching work, laborious and uncertain because of the less efficient instrumental means, could be resumed much more effectively early last year with the very efficient new Lawrence Lowell telescope specially designed for this particular problem. Some weeks ago, on plates he made with this instrument, Mr. C. W. Tombaugh, assistant on the staff, using the Blink Comparator, found a very exceptio object, which since has been stud carefully. It has been photograp regularly by Astronomer Lampland the 42-inch reflector, and also obser visually by Astronomer E. C. Slip and the writer with the large refract

The new object was first recorde the search plates of January 21 (1 23rd, and 29th, and since February has been followed closely. Besides numerous plates of it with the photographic telescope, the object been recorded on more than a sco plates with the large reflector Lampland, who is measuring both s of plates for positions of the objec rate of motion he has measured for available material at intervals betw observations with results that appe place the object outside Neptune's at an indicated distance of about 13 astronomical units...

In brightness the object is only a 15th magnitude...neither in brigh or apparent size is the o comparable with Neptune. Prelimi

It had moved across the sky! Clyde knew it could not be a star because stars seem to move very slowly over a long period of time. It must be a planet, traveling around the sun just like Earth.

On February 25, 1930, Clyde had found Planet X. He was only twenty-four years old when he made this important discovery.

14

CIVIC COURTESY AND ITS CONSEQUENCES

THE simple but expressive "Please" that turned pedestrians away from a badly trampled grass border, after all other exhortations failed, has become a classic example of the efficiency of courtesy and the gently spoken word. With this in mind, perhaps, the officials of many villages located on the route of the Lincoln Highway, and elsewhere, have erected a new sort of greeting to motorists. Instead of the usual commandatory "City Limits—Slow down to 15 miles an hour," the traveler in those parts is confronted with a cordial "——— Welcomes You." And, as if to drive home the sincerity of the sentiment, the reverse side of the sign carries, for the departing visitor, a veritable pat on the back in its friendly "Good Luck. Come Again."

This is modern Applied Psychology sure enough. For few will be the motorists who will "burn up" the roads in *those* towns, or deafen their inhabitants with wide-open cut-outs or asphyxiate them with noxious gases.

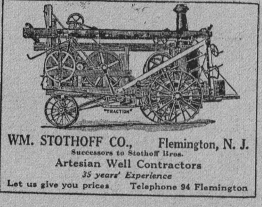
Clyde got to name the new planet. All the other planets have names of gods from ancient Greek and Roman myths. Clyde chose the name Pluto. Pluto, the ruler of the underworld, lived hidden below the Earth. Clyde thought it was the perfect name for his planet because Pluto is hidden from sight much of the time by Neptune. That is why it took him five years to find it!

Many years later, a famous museum asked
Clyde if they could have his old telescope, the one
he and his father had built. They wanted it for an
astronomy display. Did he still have it?

Yes, he had it in his backyard. But the museum
could not have it just yet. "Sorry," he said, "I am still
using it!"